T0065192

It's My Poop and You Can't Have It

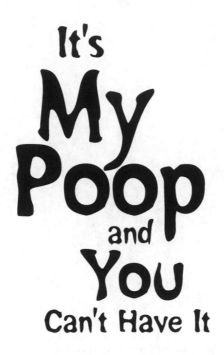

Understanding the Mind of Your Little Potty Trainer

Dr. Tallah B. and Yasmeen Brightwell

authorHOUSE®

AuthorHouse™
1663 Liberty Drive
Bloomington, IN 47403
www.authorhouse.com
Phone: 833-262-8899

Published by AuthorHouse 07/11/2023

ISBN: 978-1-7283-7792-6 (sc)
ISBN: 978-1-7283-7791-9 (e)

Library of Congress Control Number: 2023901220

Print information available on the last page.

This book is printed on acid-free paper.

JUNE IS NATIONAL POTTY-TRAINING MONTH

Dedication

This book is dedicated to our tiniest little treasures who rely on an adult ally to speak on their behalf. You little ones have a friend in ME!

Love,

Dr. B
The Mouthpiece for the Children

Contents

Introduction

Potty training should be an "I did it" moment for a child instead of a "win" for mom and dad. We grown-ups often view potty training as a task with an end date instead of a process with no right or wrong approach, as each child is different. The goal should be to assist your little one in reaching this exciting milestone in a healthy and stress-free manner.

There is no scientific evidence that describes potty-trained children as any more intellectually savvy than that of their slower-trained counterparts, as many parents believe. Most are unfamiliar with the stages of growth within early childhood so they look to family and friends to guide them, without considering that each child has his/her own genetic road map and environmental circumstances which will determine the pace of their developmental journey. Nature and Nurture working together.

Child care centers and preschools have set the standard of "age-appropriate" potty training which is enforced so that preschool teachers don't have to change diapers. Many preschools will not permit a child to advance to an older classroom (usually the three-year-old group) if they are not wearing underwear. The pressure to have a child potty-trained is then pushed down to the child, parent, and the teacher in the younger classroom to ensure that the child will be trained. While some children are prepared to train, others are not. Unfortunately, we often employ a mass approach in assessing preparedness through the use of an outdated measuring tool. A two or three-year-old who is attentive during classroom activities and is compliant, may not be given the opportunity to experience a more challenging learning environment because he is wearing diapers. As parents, we are usually anxious for our little ones to move to an older classroom so we adopt the potty-training approach implemented by our child's school instead of allowing the child to train at his own pace with assistance and encouragement. Ideally, a child care that offers a mixed-age learning experience where neither age nor potty-training would determine when class advancement is appropriate, would be most productive, but unfortunately this is not a reality as many child care centers operate according to the antiquated practice where potty-training determines whether advanced learning is permitted.

I often remind parents that children of typical development will eventually master "poop making" in the potty at a normal pace. *It's My Poop* is more than a guide to potty training. It's a resource that will help parents understand better the psychology of their little angels. This guide will uncover the mind of the toddler as they proceed through the training process, and include a discussion on the many factors involved. This book has been organized to help families of little ones accomplish the potty-training mission with ease.

The descriptions "toddlers" and "preschoolers" will be referenced separately, together, and interchangeably as both have different meanings. "Toddlers" for the purpose of this book include two-year-old children, while "preschoolers" are inclusive of children three and four-years-of-age. These are normally the two age groups that are involved in potty-training.

ONE

Mom is Ready Poop is Not

Historically, mothers were the designated parent to ensure that the children met their developmental milestones at home and school. Even though I have noticed a marked shift in parental responsibilities across gender lines over the last thirty years, Mom is still the parent most concerned about potty-training.

All three of my children were successfully potty-trained, but I don't remember the details because it was not on my list of things to do. I understood that it would be a natural occurrence and that at some point they would become successful potty-goers before kindergarten and that my boys would take longer than my daughter. Most of the boys to whom I have provided service have needed more time to move from Pull-Ups to underwear. A fact that some parents do not embrace.

If I had a dollar for every parent who erroneously described their preschooler as potty-trained, I would be a wealthy lady. The most bizarre instance was the father of an eight-month-old baby who insisted that his son was prepared to potty train. The father advised my staff that his son cried whenever he was soiled or wet and exhibited great pleasure when his diaper was changed (a typical reaction of all infants but it does not constitute potty training preparedness). This clearly was an extreme case – most of us would agree that an eight-month-old is not ready for the potty, unfortunately, I know parents of two-year-old children who are as persistent as this father, which has made my life as a child care operator extremely frustrating.

The training process with a little one should be individualized, as not all toddlers or preschoolers will realize immediate success. Our responsibilities as parents, is to adopt a style of parenting for our homes and then create a more individualized approach for each child, as they are individually unique with their own temperament.

Have you ever wondered how three children could be raised in the same household but grow to be completely different from one another as young adults? This is because even though they are from they same gene pool, their genetic make-up is arranged differently, not to mention that we really do raise each child according to their own temperament and needs. They are individuals – and that's how they should be raised. This is no different from potty-training. Each child will demonstrate the following:

- Ask to sit on the potty
- Announce that she has made poop or pee in her diaper
- Ask to have her diaper changed

These signs do not always mean that it's time to toss out the diapers, but it may however be the beginning of the potty-training process (of course there are exceptions to every rule as some children will train overnight, but most will not).

Our children are not miniature adults; rather they are little innocents who look to us for assistance, guidance, and overall protection to ensure that their feelings and emotional well-being are safeguarded.

I have seen dozens of parents cross the slippery slope of effective parenting to that which could be considered abusive, during potty-training. They implement measures that could be considered intimidating and frightening to a young child. So much is stored in their little brains, they work hard to learn rules (often in several places – school, home, and grandma's house).

Many of us have asked our older children "Why do I have to repeat myself like you're two years old?" We don't realize, but this is a relevant and meaningful question. The toddler and preschooler are learning how to listen to a request and respond appropriately, not always a fluid response. You may notice your little one pauses before reacting because she is thinking about what you asked and processing the best way to respond.

Consistent conversation with your child while asking her to complete one-step tasks help her to develop brain activity. This type of interaction will assist in the potty-training process. Oftentimes parents do not enforce boundaries within which their toddler is expected to behave, but then expect them to be able to follow potty-training cues. This unreasonable attempt becomes frustrating for both child and parent. Too much information for a young child who is unprepared can be overwhelming, and training will backfire.

While some children go from diapers to potty with ease, others need to take baby steps and that's ok. Going potty, especially poop, takes time. We mistakenly believe that if our little ones are verbal and of exceptional intelligence that they are automatically prepared to potty train, but this belief is far from the truth. Muscle control and the ability to verbalize the need to use the potty is most important.

TWO

The Great Expectations Theory

Young children have a different view of the world than do adults. The life of a child prior to potty training is divided into two parts: survival and exploration. Survival takes place in the first year of life as the little ones learn to live outside of their mom's belly. Basic needs for survival are: suckling, sleeping, eliminating, sitting up, crawling, and then walking into the stage of exploration. This time is ideal for introducing rules and boundaries. Doing so will assist the little one to understand what is safe and acceptable and what is not.

Young children aim to please and require adult supervision during their journey of exploration. Some parents allow their children to grow from one stage of development to the next without providing effective guidance and direction. Once a toddler grows into a preschooler, the parents have no control but attempts to introduce the rules after the child has grown accustom to the "no rule household." I have coined this *The Great Expectations Theory* which describes a parent's failure to enforce rules but then expects the child to become magically compliant overnight. This is an unfair expectation for which the child is being penalized.

Structure, consistency, and discipline work best for effective parenting. It's easier for children when rules are the same each day. Eventually, the rules become second nature and the little ones will know exactly what is expected of them. This attentiveness is what's needed for the potty-training setup.

Preschoolers who have been exposed to structure and discipline as toddlers will be easier to train on the potty – but at their own pace, not at the pace that Mom expects them to move. While we understand "pottying" is a natural occurrence, we may forget that we don't determine when it happens. It's the child who makes that decision; we adults are simply involved to support in the process.

We may think that once our kids are verbal, they are prepared to potty, but this is not so. Learning to use the potty is as much a physical task as it is cognitive and emotional. All three have to work together.

We learn quickly that pooping in the potty for our little ones is more difficult than making pee. Poop is a solid, a thing that is more personal to a child. No matter how much we attempt to convince them that it's safe to release their poop in the potty, they will not until THEY are prepared to do so. Remember that the process is one that is a physiological event. Each child should have the opportunity to complete the process successfully and in peace. So as the spokesperson for toddler and preschool children, I will offer you a peek into their little minds.

- **How Your Child Feels**

"I've been putting something called pee and poop into a thing called a diaper for a really long time, but now that I am learning to use the big chair in the bathroom called a potty, there is so much to do. I have to remember the feeling to 'go' and sometimes I can't tell if I have to pee, poop, or have to make a fart. I used to do all three in my diaper, but now Mommy doesn't want me to do that anymore. I get really confused."

- **What Your Child is Thinking**

"Sometimes I'm really busy playing with my friends, and I'm not sure if I have to go or if it's a trick. The other day I was in the playroom with my friends, far away from the potty."

"I kind of had to go, but I thought that I could hold it until lunchtime because if I got off of the bike that I was riding my best buddy would have taken it and I would have had to pick another bike to ride."

- **Your Child Wants to Please You**

"Even though I don't feel like using the potty chair yet, I know that it would make my Mom and Dad very happy. I want them to be very proud of me but it's a lot of work right now. They like to give me stickers when I go on the potty, but if they let me stay in Pull-Ups for a few more weeks I will give them stickers for giving me time to learn to use the potty the right way."

That cited above is how young preschoolers think. Mom and Dad view potty training as a simple function, not realizing all that it involves, especially during their child's school day. Learning how to use the potty is one function of early childhood development. Your child will accomplish many other milestones, and moving from diapers to the potty will occur as long as your child is of typical development. There is more to a preschooler than her potty going parts and the concern of mastering the potty. An entire being is attached to those parts and each play an intricate role in potty-going.

THREE

The Set up for the potty

Prior to beginning the potty process, it's important to assess if the little one is prepared to train. Here are some signs of readiness:

- Verbally able to express the need to go
- Requesting to sit on the potty
- Showing interest in the potty
- Showing excitement about wearing underwear
- Uncomfortable when wet or soiled

Here are some signs of unreadiness:

- Shows no interest in the potty when asked
- Shows no discomfort in a dirty diaper
- Cries when you suggest sitting on the potty
- Soils or wets diaper
- Anxious or nervous when placed on the potty

Once he exhibits at least three of the five signs of potty readiness, the training process should begin, keeping in mind that there could be "highs" and "lows" during the process. A "Stress free" journey should be the goal for all.

The Talk

While my approach to parenting is "old school" and more parent-directed and authoritative, my thoughts on potty-training are much more liberal. Children are in complete control as they determine whether this milestone will be accomplished with ease or not. We, as parents have absolutely no control. Those parents who position themselves as the driver of this bus will most certainly crash.

Preparing for a conversation with children about potty use will help prepare them for the big day. Preparedness puts the mind at ease, even for adults. We too suffer from anxiety when we are training for a new job or moving to a new city. It's the same for children. Slowly introducing toddlers and preschoolers to the potty will give them a sense of confidence moving forward and assure them that they are not expected to train overnight because

Mom or Dad will assist them. Instead of saying, "you have to go on the potty" you can say "We are going to help you practice using the potty and then you will be a professional potty goer. All kids go in the potty when they get older so they don't have to walk around with pee and poop in their pants."

Introduction to the Bathroom

The child being potty trained is probably familiar with the goings on in the bathroom. She most likely has watched Mom and Dad take care of their business there. You can make using the potty fun. Introduce the bathroom as though the little one has never seen it. Take him to visit each area and explain what happens there. It would be helpful if you explained the following: "This is where we keep ourselves clean. We take a shower or bath everyday to keep our bodies clean. We brush our teeth at the sink to keep our teeth and mouth free of germs. When our bodies and bottom start to feel like they need to be emptied, we put our poop and pee in the toilet so that it has somewhere to go, then when we flush the toilet and it goes down the drain."

The potty candidate can practice sitting on the potty to see what it feels like. She can be encouraged to sing songs, or you might want to provide books for her to thumb through while sitting. You can explain to her that she will know when she's finished because her belly will feel empty after she poops and that she will no longer feel the urge to push until the next time.

Wiping Clean

A discussion about wiping oneself is an important skill when becoming a master potty-goer. While it should not be a concern in the beginning stages of using the potty, explaining the practice of wiping can be had while you are wiping your little one.

This can also be an opportunity to discuss body parts and the name that you will assign to each. It's best to use the exact terminology. You can explain how waste is released. If your child is a girl you can say, "When you go pee, it comes out of your vagina. When you go poop it comes out of your bottom." Of course, if your child is a boy the explanation for releasing poop would be the same as the conversation with a little girl, but releasing pee would be discussed differently, explaining to the little boy that he has a penis and that is where the pee will come from. It is at this point when you can begin a discussion on "wiping clean".

Children age five and younger should not be expected to wipe poop because it is a difficult task. The adults in charge (whether at home or school) should be responsible for wiping a young child. Far too often have a I seen little girls wiping their bottoms after going pee. I'm sure this is because girls have been taught to wipe from the front to the back as a way to prevent the spread of germs, however, this practice can also cause the development of bacteria in the vaginal area if urine is not wiped away.

Ensuring that your child is aware of which adults will keep them wiped after potty-use is extremely important and will eliminate their feelings of anxiety. At home, they should be advised of the specified family members who will be responsible for wiping them after potty use and the same information should be provided for school.

This is a perfect opportunity to discuss with children three-years and older the importance of keeping their private parts private and that only those who are going to help them wipe clean should touch those parts (unless they are visiting the doctor). This is a scary conversation that none of us want to have with our young children, but it's best that they are made aware.

Training

All children have the right to train at his or her own pace. Those of typical development will use the toilet eventually. While a few will train in an instant, most will not. I encourage the use of Pull-Ups (disposable training pants) after diapers and before underwear. There is oftentimes resistance from parents who do not want to spend money on Pull-Ups. I remind them quickly that once we have children, some choices become less about what "we" want and more about what our children need. Pull-Ups are effective because they allow for accidents, and wearing them help children to practice pulling up and down as they are constructed more like underwear and less like diapers.

Pull-Ups should not be used in place of a diaper. In other words, the purpose is to help the child to stay dry. Once wearing Pull-Ups, the little ones should be taken to the toilet throughout the day so they can learn to be independent. While in day care, a teacher should allow children the opportunity to sit on the potty, even if they don't have the urge to pee or poop. It's most effective when a teacher allows a child that is training to practice sitting on the potty after their diaper has been changed.

If a child shows absolutely no interest in sitting on the potty, it's best that they stay in diapers as Pull-Ups are not designed to be absorbent and will quickly leak. Pull-Ups should only be used on little ones who are interested in sitting on the potty and those who are motivated to become independent potty goers.

One way that parents can assist their children in learning to use the potty is to dress them in clothing that is easy for them to manipulate, such as clothing that can be pulled up and down with ease. While it's tempting to dress our little girls in tutu skirts with leggings and our little boys with belts and suspenders, it's not practical when using the potty. Learning how to use the potty isn't as easy as it seems. The children have to learn to recognize the urge to go while also having the ability to unbuckle belts or suspenders or keep big tutus and long skirts from dipping in the toilet. Save cute accessories and fancy clothing for when they are completely trained. This is how your little one prepares for potty going:

- "Oh no! I have to go potty! I wonder if it's poop or pee?"
- "Should I tell mom or should I just go?"
- "When I'm at school will I be able to make it to the potty?"
- "What if I'm riding my favorite bike and I get off to go and my friend takes it?"
- "What if I have to go and nothing comes out?"
- "Do I have to go poop or am I having farts?"

Your older toddler must have muscle control before potty-training. Pediatricians oftentimes encourage parents to begin the potty-training process simply as a result of the child's age, when in reality, potty-training will only be mastered successfully when the child is prepared.

It appears that putting poop in the potty is more difficult for little ones than pee, as pee is a liquid and poop is a solid ----- a thing. To the young mind, it can be overwhelming to put this thing that belongs to them in the toilet and watch it flush away. A type of elimination that may be confusing to them. Explain to them that it's ok if they only pee in the potty until they are comfortable to put poop in there.

Consistency is key. Send your little one to attempt the potty every forty-five minutes or so. This helps to strengthen their ability to determine if there is a need to go. Eventually, they will be able to tell you if they need to go or not because they will have developed the cue.

Using a system of reward is also an effective approach that encourages potty use. Explain to your little one that each time he uses the potty there will be a small reward (a sticker or another small token of your choice).

FOUR

Trained

So, you think that your little one is trained and ready for those superhero underwear or fancy panties? Perhaps, but not so fast. Replacing Pull-Ups with underwear is a completely different process than simply sitting on the potty while wearing Pull-Ups. Some parents think about the financial gain of no longer having to buy Pull-Ups, but the truth is that it's cheaper to purchase Pull-Ups than having to replace soiled undergarments because their child is not prepared to stay soil free. Pressuring your little one to use the potty before they are prepared to do so will turn an enjoyable process and proud milestone into a period of frustration.

The training process shouldn't be time-stamped. Again, the focus is not when we parents are ready, it's when our little ones are prepared. If training is done in an effective manner there will be fewer problems once the child moves into underwear.

Some children wear underwear for a portion of the day and then wear Pull-Ups for the other half. This approach works for children who have difficulty recognizing the cue to go when they are outside on the playground or when sleeping. Some children may be confused when substituting their underwear for Pull-Ups but most will not have difficulty as they learn quickly the difference between the two. If a child is truly potty-trained, they will not feel comfortable when they are wet or soiled, even when wearing Pull-Ups.

Recognizing True Potty Success

Once your little one can remain dry throughout the day; soil free throughout the day; and ask to use the potty, then he or she is trained! Your little one has advanced through the training process. This is an amazing time for both of you, but the process is not yet complete. Some children will move forward quickly and not look back, while others may still need cues and reminders. It's completely normal as some kiddies require more time to master their new skill set than do others. All caregivers involved in the child's potty-training should be updated daily on their progress.

Accidents

When a newly potty-trained child does not get to the potty in time, we refer to that as an "accident." When a child misses the feels-like-I-have-to-go moment, that also is an accident. Please do not confuse having an "accident" with a child who repeatedly pees or soils himself. I've experienced this often with anxious parents whose lives and emotions are invested in their preschoolers becoming 100 percent potty-trained. If your child sits in the corner and makes pee or poop on himself, he is not ready for underwear; if she is comfortable sitting in wet or soiled underwear, then she is not prepared to leave the Pull-Ups behind. Please familiarize yourself with a child who has an "accident" and one who pees and poops in their pants because they are not fully potty-trained.

Dress for Success

The first few weeks of wearing underwear is an exciting time for your child. Our responsibility as parents is to continue to assist with this process. As mentioned earlier, this is not the time for fancy ruffles and belts. Save those outfits as a reward once your child is completely trained, it's less stress for them as they practice. As an incentive, you can take your potty-training preschooler to the store and allow them to pick out their own special clothing for when they are completely trained. This will allow the potty-trainer to feel like a real decision maker in the process.

Continued Consistency

It's important to remind your little one to pay attention to the "have to go" potty cues. Send him to sit on the potty throughout the day; as often as every 20 minutes or so. This will help him to recognize the feeling to go. It would be helpful if the same practice is adapted at preschool.

Some of the BEST potty-goers have to be reminded "to go" when they are busy at play. Those who are verbal will probably share with you their frustration about having to leave their play-time to use the potty.

FIVE

Using The Potty at Child Care

If I put a dollar in the bank for every aggravating moment that I have encountered an overly anxious parent of a potty-trainer, I would be a wealthy woman. Most of the experiences were with parents of two-year-old toddlers, who were firm believers that their child should be given a pack of underwear on their second birthday.

The first encounter in 1991 should have forewarned me of what was to come over the next thirty-years. The incident of the father who believed that his eight-month-old baby was prepared to potty-train, was one of a long list of parents who would misunderstand the potty-training process for their little ones. When I refer to the age of potty-training preparation, I am not making reference to infants (0 to 18 months old) or the older infant/ toddler (18 months – 2 years of age) as infants do not have the muscle capacity to train for the potty.

This approach to potty-training may be the same practice that is adopted at child care. When visiting centers during your selection process, inquire about the potty-training policy, even if your child is an infant, so you will be aware once your baby reaches potty-training age. The plan should always be that your infant will remain at the same center until he ages out. I have my own opinion on how best to potty train, but your thoughts may differ. A child care provider who best fits your approach and philosophy would be a wise choice. The ideal approach to training is rooted in consistency and promotes a positive training experience for the child. A child care center that fosters aggressive and harsh potty-training is unhealthy for any child.

Once your child begins the potty-training process, speak with her teacher to learn her thoughts on how best to train. Many parents forget that there is an entire classroom of children other than their own (we would love for our own child to be the focus of the teacher's attention but unfortunately, in most situations that cannot be the case). The teacher most likely has a schedule for training those who are prepared to be so.

It's best to be respectful when approaching your child's teacher to inquire about their potty-training approach, whether you agree with them or not. Respect should be the case when addressing any issue with your child's teacher or child care provider. It's difficult to understand how some parents are disrespectful to those who care for their children in any capacity. When addressing potty-training concerns however, first question about the policy if you have not done so prior to enrolling your child. If you are familiar with the center's approach to potty-training but are concerned with your child's individual progress or lack thereof, ensure that your concerns are stated in a tactful manner so that the teacher does not feel insulted. There are many factors that must be considered when potty-training a little one at child care, as there are more distractions that occur than do at home. There are other children arriving and departing at different times throughout the day (young children like to people watch) in addition to daily activities, there are many other distractions which may result in a different training experience than at home.

Don't assume that your child is prepared to use the potty at school simply because she has shown interest at home. Some children train simultaneously, at home and school; some train at home first; others train at school first. It's difficult to predict until the process begins. A "potty-training candidate" must have some language. If a child is not somewhat verbal it makes it virtually impossible for a teacher to know when he has to use the potty. Encouraging the use of words as early as twelve-months-old can contribute to easier potty-training as the child will be able to verbalize if they are prepared to use the potty or not, but remember that an intellectually savvy child does not necessarily mean that they are ready.

While many parents do believe that their child will train naturally in every setting, this is simply not the case. There should be a collaborative an orchestrated effort between home, school, and anywhere else that the potty-trainer spends time. One approach that a parent can use is to accompany the little one to the potty upon arrival to child care or grandma's house and explain that she should do the same thing on the potty "there" as she does at home. This will provide her with confirmation that those at the center or at grandma's house understand that she is learning to use the potty and that an appointed adult will assist in your absence. This practice will create a situation that is less stressful for the potty-trainer.

Currently, I have a three-year-old child enrolled in my preschool program who has mastered potty-training at school but not at home. This little fella feels a sense of pride at school as his accomplishment has earned him the title of class leader. He is the first of all the children in his class to wear Pull-Ups and to use the potty throughout the day. Unfortunately, he is not as eager at home, and that's ok. Mom and dad are accepting of this and simply continue to encourage him.

SIX

The Nightmare Parent

It has been disheartening to watch hundreds of little ones traumatized by overanxious and misinformed parents who push potty training on them when they are unprepared to begin the process. This aggressiveness from Mom and Dad can cause the child to feel anxious and overwhelmed; in some cases, it can cause the child to regress. There is no rule in the area of child development that requires a toddler to be in underwear by age two.

The natural order of potty-training should not be a painful and frustrating process, but it is often reduced to such, when the adults involved fail to realize that their function is to assist in the process and not to takeover completely. No matter how prepared Mom and Dad are for their little one to train, he will determine when it's time to do so.

Some parents have difficulty with a potty-training philosophy that is child-directed instead of directed by the adult. The belief is that the child is taking control of a situation that should be for the parent. This is my belief when discipline is involved, but not for potty-training. My approach to child-rearing is holistic in that I consider the whole child in every situation. Potty-training is not simply a separate function, disconnected from the way a child thinks and feels. My philosophy is open for debate of course, as many parents adhere to the advice from their pediatrician who may encourage potty-training their little one prematurely. Unless a physician is a Developmental Pediatrician, he or she has not had extensive studies in early childhood development. Their focus is understanding young children from a medical point of view. In most cases, your child's provider at child care will not be formally trained in early childhood development, but they may have hands-on experience in the potty-training process. Their advice to parents may be more effective than information provided by the medical professional.

The function of a teacher or child care provider can be quite challenging. Cultivating a pleasant working relationship with parents is not always easy. In fact, I find this to be the most draining duty of my responsibilities, as not all parents are rational – or even likeable for that matter. Below are several of my most challenging moments:

The Brothers Who Were Too Beautiful to Discipline

This will sound unbelievable, but unfortunately these series of events really happened. A mother of two poorly behaved boys advised me that her children were "too beautiful to discipline" when I requested that she enforce a method of parenting that would address their behavior as it jeopardized the safety of others and that of their own. While this mother expressed her beliefs that her boys were "extra" attractive, she was most proud of the physical appearance of her youngest son as his hair was blonder and his eyes bluer than his brother's. This Mom would provide the younger boy more attention at drop-of and pick-up and even post pictures of the younger boy on her social media page, excluding the older child. One could only imagine the psychological trauma of one child feeling less important than a sibling, at such a young age.

I found this experience to be more disturbing than the dad with the eight-month-old baby that he believed to be prepared for potty-training. The children of this particular parent were so aggressive that they would arrive to school with bruises on their arms and legs from fighting with one another at home. Their unacceptable behavior would cause harm to the other children in their classrooms as well. On numerous occasions, they hit the others with wooden blocks and other objects while both mom and dad were present. Instead of reprimanding this anti sociable behavior the parents would sing "Criss-cross applesauce time to cross your hands." Similar poor behavior was illustrated when the boys attended birthday parties of the other children. The "Beautiful boys" would hit, kick, and pull the hair of their classmates as mom and dad looked on. After witnessing this poor behavior, several parents terminated preschool school services due to concerns that their children were not safe in the presence of the "BeautifulBrothers".

Imagine attempting to potty-train children with such poor behavior. Of course, Mom was insistent about potty-training prematurely. The older brother however, was not interested in training at all. Mom understood this and did not force the issue, as she was aware that he did not comply with basic requests, so attempting to encourage potty-training was impossible. The younger "more attractive" child through the eyes of Mom, was a different story. Her approach to training this brother was different than the approach implemented with the older child. Mom viewed the younger boy as more intelligent than the older boy, even though both were not easy to manage. The younger child was given more freedom to defy the rules at home, causing potty-training to be extremely difficult. Mom demanded that the two-year-old be permitted to wear underwear upon arrival at school and keep them on all day. She would provide a bag full of clothing and instruct the teachers to change him throughout the day if he soiled or wet himself even though it was against the potty-training policy, of which Mom was aware. The little boy was so anxious about using the potty that he would sit on the floor to pee and poop then run from the teacher yelling when she attempted to take him to the bathroom.

A child who is poorly behaved and undisciplined prior to potty-training will exhibit the same behavior during the training process. Children require boundaries, generally speaking. The parents who deny their children such guidelines are doing them a disservice. As you might imagine, the relationship with this particular family did not end well. In fact, I terminated service and refunded their full tuition payment.

Twins

I have had dozens of twins enrolled over the last thirty-years, but the parents of only one set understood that each twin was their own person and may not necessarily meet each milestone in sync with his sibling. The families of all of the other twins however, believed that their twins would grow in exactly the same manner, reach every single milestone on the same day, and have the same needs.

The Mom of one set of twins was the most difficult and irrational parent of the entire group. Her twins were two-year-old girls. One was quiet and withdrawn and the other was outgoing, verbal, and very personable. The outgoing twin commanded the most attention. She was even neatly dressed as the withdrawn twin was not. The more sociable twin was the first to be greeted by Mom, Dad, or other family members when they arrived for pick-up. I directed the staff to make an extra effort to greet both girls simultaneously during morning drop-off so the shy twin would not feel left out. Mom was in complete disagreement with my observation and continued her same routine with greeting the girls one by one as she arrived, ignoring the fact that the withdrawn twin felt left out as her sister received the most attention when they were picked-up. The twin with the larger personality was permitted to be in front while her shy sister stood behind and looked on as a spectator. Guess what happened when it was time to potty-train? You guessed right. The outgoing twin would succeed and the withdrawn twin would not.

The outgoing twin was prepared to train. She was excited, motivated, and understood that she would be permitted to wear panties if she used the potty. The shy twin would become extremely emotional when she was placed on the potty. Both girls began training at the same time because Mom wanted both to train together for her own convenience.

Each morning when the girls arrived, the outgoing twin would announce that she wanted to sit on the potty. Her sister was not interested at all. Mom advised the staff that once the shy twin had time to observe her more outgoing sister potty-training, she too would show interest in training also. I thought to myself *"ok if you say so."*

In most potty-training cases there are more moving parts than simply potty training. This was clear in the case of these twins. The shy, somewhat withdrawn sister was not as friendly and received less attention than her twin. Learning to use the potty required time, patience, and understanding from Mom, Dad, and all those involved in the training process. This little one needed extra time to overcome her shyness and to figure out where she fit in both at home and school.

Several weeks after training began, the outgoing sister was ready for panties. She kept her Pull-Ups dry for the entire day and asked to use the potty when she was in need. She did not use Pull-Ups as a diaper, and she didn't like to be wet or soiled. She was ready for panties.

Her twin, however, was not one bit interested. Mom tried to convince me that both sisters should wear panties. She didn't want the shy twin to feel excluded, even though the child became anxious and emotional whenever she was asked to sit on the potty. Whenever Mom arrived for pick-up, she would praise the outgoing twin for staying dry and remind the shy twin that she too could be a big girl like her sister if only she would sit on the potty.

While observing the developmental progress of young children is completely fascinating, it is also extremely frustrating to witness such reckless interference in that natural progression from controlling parents. Interference that could possibly result in an anxious and angry little child. This Mom will one day regret her choice to praise one of her twin girls over the other, this will surely become a disastrous situation.

It is difficult for me as a child care provider to interfere with a parent's approach to parenting. I can imagine that parenting twins is challenging for any parent, but its imperative to view each child as an individual. Continually comparing one to the other can create a bigger set of problems. In this particular situation, my concern was that the shy twin would regress in other areas of development and may feel a sense of inability and failure, so I gave her extra attention and encouraged the teachers to do so as well. I separated her from her sister and ensured that she interacted with the other children during free-play so that she would feel a sense of independency. Each week we noticed marked growth with the shy sister and her excitement to interact with her friends. She was taking the initiative to play with others and was no longer confined to the direction and rules of her more outgoing sister. After several months, the shy twin became her own person and moved from diapers to Pull-Ups and finally to panties.

Precious Three-Year-Old Sassy

Sassy was one of the most extreme cases of "potty rebellion" and regression that I have ever witnessed. This three-year-old angel was always dressed in big skirts with lots of tulle, white tights, and shiny black patent leather shoes. She was the youngest of three, and the only girl. The older siblings were two boys who were poorly behaved, so while Sassy's behavior was mostly normal, she sometimes would imitate the poor behavior of her brothers. Occasionally, it would be difficult for the teachers to discipline her because she did not understand rules and boundaries as they were not enforced at home.

One day, Dad marched into Sassy's classroom and ordered her teacher that she should begin to place Sassy on the potty throughout the day. He believed that her "sassy" attitude and precocious demeanor qualified her for potty candidacy. He would be in for the rudest of awakenings.

The battle began when Mom and Dad forced Sassy into Pull-Ups. She did not want to wear them and let it be known as she would ask the teachers to replace her Pull-Ups with diapers. This was not an option for her parents, particularly Dad. He reminded us to keep the Pull-Ups on her during the day and to ensure that she was taken to sit on the potty. He directed the teachers to place her in time-out if she defied the potty-rule, but we of course advised him that we could not enforce such extreme discipline for Sassy's failure to use the potty.

By Sassy's third day in Pull-Ups, she began to remove it and poop and pee on the floor. This typically developing child was in the beginning stages of problematic behavior, simply because she was not prepared to potty-train. The struggle that she had with her parents at home would begin every morning and continue through bedtime (according to the reports provided by Mom). Both parents had difficulty understanding why Sassy was so defiant. They believed that since both of the older brothers had trained without problems, Sassy should as well. Dad argued that he would not allow a two-year-old to make "household decisions" even though this was not a household decision I thought to myself. This was about little Sassy not being ready to potty train. In fact, it seemed odd to me that there were no rules or boundaries for these children otherwise and that ensuring that this child was potty-trained was more important than encouraging socially acceptable behavior. Mom and Dad were steadfast in their determination to win this battle. However, my potty-training policy interfered in their plan. We required that Sassy wear diapers at school, as she would poop and pee in the Pull-Ups causing it to leak since it is not as absorbent as diapers.

According to Mom and Dad, Sassy was not given treats at home as punishment for not using the potty. They advised us that she was not to participate in any parties at school or be allowed to engage in show and tell with the other children. While this form of punishment made Sassy feel horrible, it was the fancy dresses that Mom and Dad would not allow her to wear that seem to make her feel worse. She didn't cry when Dad reminded us to exclude her from activities (which we did not). However, when he pointed out that she was wearing jeans and sneakers as a punishment, she would cry uncontrollably. It was heartbreaking to watch this little girl become angry and withdrawn simply because she did not want to potty-train.

By the age of four, Sassy had progressed to Pull-Ups, but still would not sit on the potty. The daily battle continued as she was completely uninterested. She would fight her Mom and Dad each day in protest. The teachers tried using stickers, praise, and treats to encourage her, but the damage done by her parents at home, overpowered any positive reinforcement at school.

Sassy declared war on Mom and Dad once she turned five years-old. It was them against her. She eventually began to pee and poop in the potty at school but not at home. She even began to wear panties at school but would intentionally wet and poop in them when she was with Mom or Dad.

The events that unfolded could have been prevented if Sassy was permitted to train at her pace. Unfortunately, two months before Sassy was to advance to kindergarten, the family relocated out of State, so I am unsure how the situation with Sassy ended but I am confident that the struggle persisted.

Two-and-a-Half-Year-Old Sanford

This little charmer was the cutest little guy. He had perfect manners and knew which adults that he could manipulate. While his behavior was manageable at school, Mom and Dad had extreme difficulty controlling little Sanford at home. The failure to implement boundaries and discipline at home interfered with Sanford's ability to maximize his fullest potential at school because he was not accustomed to respecting figures of authority. This caused him great confusion.

Occasionally, Dad would attempt to discipline Sanford but he was not consistent, so Sanford was unsure of which commands to respond. Sometimes Dad would allow him to stand on the table and sometimes he would not. Sanford's behavior with Mom was completely over the top and unacceptable. When Mom arrived for pick-up in the evenings he would run, throw toys, and slap her in the face. Rather than correct Sanford's behavior and enforce some form of discipline, Mom would laugh.

By Sanford's third birthday it was clear that he was in no shape to potty train. Mom was irritated that her little fella was not at all interested in the potty. She would attempt to encourage him, but he would yell *"No! I don't want to!"*

Mom complained that she couldn't understand why Sanford was not progressing like his peers. This little fella was not interested in the potty, but he also was not interested in doing much of anything other than playing by himself, isolated in the corner away from the other children. He also was not interested in participating in teacher-directed activities. The teachers would encourage him to join the group but he would ignore their request. It was disheartening to watch this little boy become withdrawn as the ineffective approach to parenting interfered with his natural ability to thrive. Appropriate behavior is the foundation for developmental growth. Children require guidance from the adults in their lives.

Mom requested that we place Sanford on the potty during the day. Not only was he not interested in the potty, he would ask the teachers to put him in a diaper instead of a Pull-Up. The Pull-Up was a reminder of his responsibility to potty-train, of which he was completely against. This defiant attitude continued when Sanford began preschool. Our efforts were in vain, as he used the Pull-Ups to pee and poop.

By age four, this little charmer had not progressed much. Mom advised us that he was indeed potty-trained at home. This was a fairytale, as he was NOT trained at all. This Mom expected the teachers at school to train him as it was too difficult for her. He was completely comfortable wearing a wet and soiled Pull-Up during the day because he was permitted to do so at home. One of the concerns that I expressed to Mom was that Sanford would not ask to use the potty. He would poop in his pants while playing and only admit to having gone if asked. Remember *the Great Expectation Theory*? This is a perfect example. Sanford's parents failed to discipline and direct him when he was a toddler. As a preschooler, his Mom and Dad had great difficulty with him, and rather than correct it, they fostered his inappropriate conduct. Eventually his parents realized that Sanford's behavior was no longer "cute" and they became frustrated during their attempt to unravel three-years of poor behavior.

As with any of the other parents, we would not appease Sanford's Mom and her request to allow him to wear underwear until he was prepared to do so. She had to allow us to potty-train Sanford according to our policy. He would slowly but surely become a successful potty-trainer.

Sweet Two-and-a-Half-Year-Old Girl

Cutie-Pie was as quiet as a mouse. While she was extremely verbal, she was selective about it, and chose to be silent at school only talking to friends during play time when extremely necessary.

She also would not participate in circle-time even though she understood all that was being discussed as she would describe her entire day with mom when she arrived for pick-up. A new baby in the home also created a new set of circumstances for little Cutie-Pie.

When Cutie-Pie returned from school after the COVID shutdown, it was as though she were starting all over. She was extremely withdrawn and unhappy to return. On her first day, Mom requested that we allow Cutie-Pie the opportunity to use the potty. Mom advised that Cutie-Pie would request to go poop and pee when asked. I thought to myself *"this is not going to happen."* This child was extremely shy prior to being at home for several months. There was no way that she would be prepared to potty-train at school as she had regressed overall. Additionally, Mom treated Cutie-Pie like a baby but expected "BIG GIRL" behavior.

The first week, we allowed Cutie Pie to wear panties. Each day, she would sit in the corner and pee. The teachers would attempt to place her on the potty every thirty minutes or so, but there was no action. She would wait until she was in panties

47

and then poop and pee. We advised Mom that Cutie-Pie needed to wear a Pull-Up. Hesitant, Mom agreed. She was concerned that Cutie-Pie would regress, which I couldn't understand because she had already exhibited overall marked regression. There were many moving parts to this situation. To begin, the little girl was already shy; had a new baby in the house; had a mother who treated *her* like an infant; was not verbal at school; wore huge ruffled skirts; and was not prepared to use the potty at school.

After two months of consistency and encouragement, Cutie-Pie was able to stay dry in her Pull-Ups. The teacher would put her in panties for the first part of the day after ensuring that she would remain dry. Once she mastered the potty in the morning for a period of time, she was permitted to wear panties for the full day. Cutie-Pie was still very shy and not as verbal at school as we would have liked, but she grew comfortable with whispering quietly to her teacher when she needed to use the potty.

Mom finally understood the big picture. She was pleased with Cutie-Pie's smooth transition to the potty and realized that it was a process that required her to consider her child's feelings and not her own.

My Eighteen-Month-Old Pumpkinseed

I am the proud mother of three "little angels" who were once preschoolers. My princess, Pumpkin has always looked up to her two older brothers. Whatever they did, she followed, back then and to the present day.

When she was eighteen-months old she watched her brothers use the potty. She decided that she wanted to do the same. Dad and I were not in a hurry to potty-train Pumpkin. We were not aggressive potty trainers, even with the brothers. We allowed them to train when they were ready. In fact, the older brother required Pull-Ups at bedtime well into his fifth birthday. The process was so unimportant to us that I don't even remember moving them from Pull-Ups to underwear.

Pumpkin would run to the potty every time she felt the need to go, especially when one of the brothers were in the bathroom. She would sit on the potty and poop and pee but only when she wanted to, not consistently. If we asked her if she wanted to pee on the potty, she would yell a firm "NO!"

After a month or so of potty using, she was on to the next venture, completely uninterested in the bathroom or training. We packed up the Pull-Ups and went back to diapers. We understood that her interest was a phase and that this was not her time to potty-train. She would not become completely potty-trained until the age of three. Eighteen-month-old babies are not prepared to potty train. They cannot grasp the basic understanding of potty use, as they do not have the attentiveness or sustainability to be permanently trained.

On more than several occasions, I have had parents request that we assist their young toddler (under the age of two) with potty training. My response has always been the same, "Unfortunately we cannot." Over a thirty-year period, I have never encountered a toddler under the age of two who demonstrated potty-training preparedness. Little ones at this age have so much to explore, and have other tasks on which to focus. Why would a parent spend time forcing an unprepared child to potty-train during a stage of development filed with so much more to learn and experience?

SEVEN

Establishing Boundaries and Enforcing Methods of Discipline

As mentioned in the earlier chapters, incorporating effective measures of discipline within the practices of parenting is key to successfully potty training, and helping your little one to become a well-behaved child who behaves in a manner that is socially acceptable.

As an old-school educator and parent, it is gut-wrenching for me to see little ones behaving in a manner that is completely unacceptable and disrespectful to figures of authority, particularly to their own parents. Over the last twenty years, I have witnessed a decline in effective parenting. Two and three-year-old children seem to be the head of their households as they dismiss simple requests from their parents and do not follow basic directions. This behavior is oftentimes condoned.

We often dismiss such unacceptable behavior from our toddlers as indicative of the "terrible twos." I have never accepted this school of thought as it seems to be an excuse for parents to abandon the implementation of effective discipline. There are the "terribles" in every stage of development, so to focus simply on the age of "two" and determine that poor behavior is normal because they are "two-years-old" is counterproductive and interferes in the healthy behavioral growth of the child. Parents are their children's first teachers, so it's their responsibility to encourage good behavior and redirect or reprimand behavior which is poor.

Early childhood is the shortest stage during a child's life but yet the most important. The foundation created by Parents will determine how a child develops. The approach to parenting should be rooted in discipline, but fit each household according to the morals and values adopted. My theory however, is broader than one simple style of parenting.

Implementing an effective approach to childrearing with one child is not as difficult as with two or more. Parents may believe that there is a one-size-fits-all style of parenting, but this is not the case. While one basic parenting style can lead the household and set rules, there also should be a substyle that is fluid and can be applied to each child individually.

As an example, one can consider a household with two children. Child number one, a four-year-old boy, is the oldest of two children. He is extremely active and has difficulty following rules at home and at school. Time-out is implemented as are removal of privileges such as watching television and using electronic devices. Child number two is a three-year-old girl. She is generally compliant; has occasional outbursts at home and school, but is easily managed with a warning. Discipline for this child does not warrant the same approach as applied to the older child. He required discipline that was firm because it was warranted. The behavioral outcome of both children will be successful due to specific parenting that is designed to address individual behavior.

This same theory should be applied when assisting in the potty-training process. Each child will train differently. One child may master the potty with ease at age two, while a sibling may have more difficulty and require prompting. Keep in mind that our responsibility as parents is assisting our children to reach specified milestones with patience and love without intimidation. Providing a safe and loving home with rules and boundaries will allow your child to be the best that he or she can be.

EIGHT

Potty-training your Child with Special Needs

Parents of young children with special needs, often attempt to potty-train without considering that their child's delay may interfere with their ability to potty-train at the same pace as typically developing children. My advice is to first address the need that requires extra assistance so that the child can reach age-appropriate developmental milestones, then begin potty-training. It is imperative that the behavioral and cognitive opportunities for these children are not being compromised because the focus is on potty training.

I have always been a proponent of an individualized approach to development for all young children regardless of ability, but I am particularly vocal when speaking on behalf of children with challenges, as there may be unreasonable expectations for them to progress according to a time-line meant for a child of typical development. The reason for such expectation may vary. The parent of a child with special needs may be in denial about their challenges and feel that their child should progress at the same pace as children of typical development. Another theory could be that the parents of a child with challenges may not be in denial of their child's special needs, but may have pressure from the child's school to potty-train.

Regardless of outside influences, parents of this population should remember that they are the advocates for their children. The primary focus should always be the children's emotional health and well-being as feelings of insecurities may interfere with their overall emotional growth, potentially resulting in behavioral problems.

Oftentimes, parents may consult with their pediatrician for assistance, unaware that most pediatricians do not have extensive training in early childhood psychology. Pediatricians often provide helpful medical advice but that may not be helpful for the developmental growth of a child with special needs. In such a situation, the pediatrician should recommend a developmental expert to provide assistance. The child's needs should determine the level of expectations for meeting various milestones. A child who does not have typical development, may be high-functioning and able to accomplish some age-appropriate tasks. It is the responsibility of the parent to provide a clear picture of their child to the health care provider and other experts so that the child can receive the help that's needed.

Experts who are well trained in the area of early childhood development can provide parents with the guidance needed to assist their child to realize their fullest potential. The expert will remind parents to prioritize the goals that are important for their child --- not for themselves. While learning how to use the potty is necessary, tackling challenges such as behavior, interacting socially, and participating in group activities should be more of a concern, as these areas have a direct impact on overall emotional well-being and self-image (most important). If your child is having social difficulty interacting with other children, the focus should be on how best to encourage acceptable behavior so that other children will enjoy play-time with your child instead of rejecting him.

A child's level of functioning usually will determine the associated behaviors and tendencies that accompany the specific diagnosis. I always advise parent to discourage unwanted behaviors, even if some behaviors are typical for specified challenges, for example: children diagnosed with autism display self-stimulatory behavior such as hand flapping or other rapid hand movement. The goal however, is to assist the child to behave as typically and independent as possible. Once such goals are accomplished, there can be a focus on potty-training.

NINE

Overall Parenting During and Post Covid-19

The fallout from the novel coronavirus has been devastating in a global sense. Many of us have never experienced a pandemic, but our children (Age five through young adults) will be able to say that they have. They will be forever impacted by the unexpected interference in their young lives. What should have been their normal journey of childhood has been altered to a *Twilight Zone* episode, similar to the reality show *Survivor*. The basic milestones that I expected from my boys who were preschoolers in late 1990 and early 2000's have changed drastically. This is also true for school aged children and young adults. My teenage daughter began her first year of high school in the fall of 2019. She was in school for 6 months, only to be isolated at a home for the following 18 months due to the health state of emergency. None of us could have prepared ourselves or our children for the overwhelming stress and sense of helplessness that would occur during and after the pandemic. The unknown, has triggered anxiety for children who previously hadn't experienced coping difficulties prior to COVID.

I have never witnessed the widespread regression and behavioral difficulty in young children that I am experiencing since the Covid-19 shutdown. It is disturbing to witness. I am unsure if I am witnessing the results from young children spending long-term periods at home with parents who didn't enforce structure throughout the day, or if the long-term distraction in their normal routines have resulted in such behavior. Either way, we will experience the fallout from this devastation for years to come.

I advise parents to focus on their own emotional well-being, in addition to that of their children. Mom and Dad must be in a healthy emotional state before they can assist their children. Parents are required to function at a higher level of happiness, as young children internalize the mood of those adults with whom they spend time, whether it's their parents or caregiver. They are forming attachments to those around them and eventually imitate their behaviors. The mission during any such health state of emergency is to attempt to create a home life that is as normal as possible.

Several of the children returning to my preschool program after the COVID shutdown suffered from separation anxiety and an overall anxiousness of becoming ill. During the shutdown, parents of children with special needs reported an increase of poor behavior. While I encourage the continuation of effective discipline, I also advised that parents should be more understanding and institute an approach to parenting that allows for more patience. Children who were enrolled in child care or preschool may have exhibited marked changes in behavior because their normal routine was disrupted; including the inability to visit with grandparents, other relatives, and friends with whom they were accustomed to seeing.

While young children are resilient, it is still critical that parents observe their children so that they can intervene in the development of anti-social behavior or mood changes that reflect feelings of sadness. There are many ways to entertain and stimulate young children who are not attending an early educational program for whatever reason. As of today, there are no confirmed studies that prove that the preschool population has contracted or contributed to the spread of COVID-19 at high percentage rates.

As reported by the Mayo Clinic, most young children who were infected with COVID-19 typically don't become as sick as adults and some may not show any symptoms at all. Additionally, the American Academy of Pediatrics and the Children's Hospital Association reported that children in the U.S. represents about 16 % of all COVID-19 cases. Preschool and child care is where your little one interacts with friends and bonds with their surrogate parents who will introduce them to the world outside of the home. Social interaction is as important as scholastic achievement.

While I understand that some parents have concerns about the health safety of their toddlers while in school, it is imperative to do your own research and come to your own conclusion. We must all rely on our ability to think critically about

COVID and the minimal effects that it has had on young children. If you do choose to keep your child home due to the concerns over COVID and any other pandemic coming our way, attempt to create a learning and social-pod with other families who have children the same age as your own. Develop your own regulations for the best health practices to ensure that those in attendance are healthy as to decrease the spread of unwanted germs. The social time should be scheduled for three or four times a week for at least an hour. This type of routine will allow your child to experience a somewhat normal childhood during an abnormal time in their young lives.

TEN

Effective Potty-training
in a Nutshell

Potty-training is a natural occurrence that all children of typical development will master prior to beginning kindergarten. A successful and permanent potty-goer requires strong muscles, as well as a consistent routine and guidance from the adults involved. Parents cannot expect success if they haven't implemented a structured environment within the household.

While some children will complete the process with ease, others will take longer and require encouragement, assistance, and rewards to promote potty success. These same little ones may need to wear Pull-Ups as an "accident-catcher" while learning how to recognize the need to go. Their processing and assessing the situation includes holding their internal muscles, while pausing play to think about which potty rules apply when they are away from home.

The beginning of the process should not be determined by the economic freedom of diapers, Pull-Ups, or the convenience of not having to change a dirty bottom. It should be based upon whether your child can understand and complete the training process stress-free. This is what matters most. Some parents erroneously believe that potty-traning is associated with intelligence. It is disheartening to me that some continue to traumatize their fragile children as they apply an outdated practice of potty-training in an attempt to ensure that their little ones are trained by age two.

While many of us often allow friends and family to advise us on how best to potty-train our children, more often than not, they are advising based upon their experiences. This practice coupled with pressure from preschools result in disaster. The practice from child care centers and other early childhood programs that require a child to be out of diapers before advancing to the next level of learning is counterproductive. This interferes with a child's ability to thrive according to his scholastic ability. Parents should consider this practice before selecting a child care program. My practice of potty-training is not based upon any ground breaking science, but rather relies on a practical approach. My philosophy however, is in total disagreement with the outdated practice of classroom placement according to toileting ability.

A healthy approach to potty-training should begin before the process is even considered, through the use of effective discipline that includes boundaries and the respect for figures of authority. This practice will keep young children safe while also preparing them to follow directions needed for effective potty-training. Poor behavior that is permitted to continue over the age of three will not simply dissipate because parents are prepared to rid their preschooler of diapers. Your child is the most important participant in this process --- he or she will most surely be a successful "potty-goer" by the time kindergarten begins.

DEAR MOMMY, DADDY, GRANDMA, AUNTIE, AND TEACHER:

THANK YOU FOR READING THE STUFF IN THIS BOOK. I THINK THE LADY IS ON TO SOMETHING. I KNOW YOU GUYS ARE HAPPY THAT I TURNED TWO-YEARS-OLD BECAUSE YOU WANT ME TO WEAR THE COOL UNDERWEAR YOU GOT. I LIKE THEM 'CAUSE THEY HAVE MY FAVORITE CARTOON CHARACTER ON THEM, BUT I DON'T THINK THAT I SHOULD WEAR THEM YET BECAUSE I'M NOT SURE I CAN GO ON THE POTTY YET.

THERE IS SO MUCH TO REMEMBER. I HAVE TO KNOW WHEN TO GO WHILE I'M AT HOME; EATING MY FAVORITE CEREAL; OR WHEN I'M AT SCHOOL, THE HARDEST PLACE TO REMEMBER TO GO POTTY 'CAUSE THERE IS SO MUCH HAPPENING AROUND ME. LOTS OF STUFF TO WATCH. I DON'T DO A GOOD JOB SHARING MY TOYS YET, SO I DON'T THINK I'M READY TO GO TO POTTY EVERYTIME. I THINK ABOUT WHO WOULD TAKE MY FAVORITE TOY IF I HAD TO RUN TO THE POTTY. OR HOW LONG IT WOULD TAKE ME TO ASK THE TEACHER TO GO TO THE POTTY. OR HOW LONG IT WOULD TAKE ME TO RUN DOWN THE HALL. OR HOW LONG IT WILL TAKE ME TO TAKE OFF

MY BELT. SHOULD I ASK BEFORE I FEEL LIKE I HAVE TO GO? OR SHOULD I ASK RIGHT WHEN I THINK I HAVE TO GO? I MIGHT NOT REMEMBER ALL THESE THINGS YET, SO THAT'S WHY IT'S BETTER TO LET ME PRACTICE FIRST. I CAN WORK A LITTLE BIT AT A TIME AND WORK ON KNOWING THE FEELING THAT WILL TELL ME WHEN TO GO. THAT WOULD BE BETTER 'CAUSE I CAN JUST WORK ON SHARING INSTEAD. THAT WAY, I WON'T BE SO SAD IF I MESS UP MY COOL UNDERWEAR. BESIDES, I'M GONNA POOP IN THE POTTY BEFORE I GO TO BIG BOYS' SCHOOL. I PROMISE.

LOVE,
YOUR KID

The Story
of
Pumpkin and the Potty
You Can Do It!
Yes You Can

Now that you are 2½ years old, I want to talk to you about the bathroom. We don't only use this room to take a bath and brush our teeth, we use it to put our poop and pee in the potty because we can't keep it in our pants forever. When you are ready you can sit on the potty and I will give you stickers and treats.

(1)

I really love all of those treats that my mom talked about. Maybe going poop on the potty won't be so bad. I won't have to carry the poop and pee in my pants anymore.

②

I'm doing it... sitting on the potty. It's not so bad it's kind of fun. I think it's better than having poop on me.

③

I'm ready for the potty
Because I'm a big girl!

④

About the Author

Dr. Attallah Brightwell is an Early Educational Psychologist, Behavioral Specialist, and Paralegal. The owner/operator of several child development centers, Dr. Brightwell has been the voice of young children since 1991. Her first center provided services to at risk preschoolers including those with behavioral and developmental challenges along with typically developing children. Her work with autistic children during this time placed her as a pioneer in the field, as she created a style of teaching that promoted learning for this specific population of preschoolers long before many in the medical and psychological communities were familiar with the condition. Dr. Brightwell's graduate school thesis published in 1995 was an observational research study that followed and documented the cognitive growth of an autistic preschooler over a period of two years (Five years prior to the child being officially diagnosed by a team of psychologists).

As an advocate for individualism, Dr. Brightwell's approach to assisting in the development of the young is based upon the belief that most children are educable if enrolled in a child care program that is loving, clean, safe and stimulating where each child has the opportunity to develop at his/her own pace, the same ideology adopted for potty-training.

Dr. Brightwell's experience coupled with her formal educational training is unmatched in the child care industry allowing her to develop the most effective approach to assisting young children to maximize their fullest potential, regardless of race, gender, socio-economic status or developmental challenges.

Yasmeen Rose Brightwell is the youngest child and only daughter of Dr. Brightwell. A high school scholar/ athlete and former student volunteer at her mother's child development center, Yasmeen encouraged her mom to put her potty–training experience and expertise into text by writing this book. She too wanted to contribute her observation as a volunteer and friend to the children. Her job as a storyteller, activities director, and circle-time leader exposed her to the miserable truth of how awful some toddlers and preschoolers feel when they are forced to potty-train when unprepared to do so. She observed the struggle that both her mother and the teachers encountered with parents who pushed their toddlers into training when they were not ready, not to mention how horrible she felt watching the frustration of the little ones. Yasmeen created a reward system for all of the children who willingly attempted to go with the teacher to the potty whether they were successful once in the potty room or not. Yasmeen believed that all of the children should feel like winners.

Printed in the United States
by Baker & Taylor Publisher Services